Karl Schulz

Content and Essence of German God-Belief

Originally Printed as the 2nd volume of
The God-Believing German

Imprimerie Ville de Papier, Cincinnati, O.
2022

Originally published in Germany, 1939, by Richard Queißer Verlag, Jauer in Schlesien.
Printing: Richard Quießer printing house, formerly Jauer's Tageblatt printing company Jauer i. Schlef.

Note on United States English Translation:
Under US law, the person who creates the translation secures copyright to the translated work, assuming that either (1) *an existing translation does not already have copyright*, or (2) the new translation is substantially different from an existing translation under copyright. The original work has since lapsed in its copyright, however all rights are reserved for this translation.

**Translated to English by Siria
September - November 2022
2022 © Imprimerie Ville de Papier**

Printed in the United States of America
First Published Edition – January 2023
ISBN 978-1-7370610-6-9

CONTENT AND ESSENCE OF GERMAN GOD-BELIEF

1. The Main Focus of the German Belief in God, is God— 11

2. German Belief in God Wants the Unity of Our People in True Faith to the Race— 20

3. German Belief in God Requires No Mediation— 24

4. German Belief in God Sees the Way to the Unity of Faith of Our People in Completely Overcoming Christianity— 27

5. German Belief in God Stands in Awe of Death— 33

6. German Belief in God Opposes Doctrine of Original Sin- 43

7. According to German Belief in God, the National Community is the Highest & Only Community, Rejecting the Priesthood- 45

8. The German Belief in God Professes the Morality of Duty and Proves Itself In Service to Our People — 46

9. German Belief in God Includes a Belief in Fact that Finds Visible Expression in the Way of Life — 48

10. German Belief in God Recognizes Divine Work in the History of Our People & Builds on High Images of the Germanic Race- 49

11. German Belief in God Strives for Celebration of Faith in Naming Ceremonies, Marriages, and Honoring the Dead — 52

12. German Belief in God Wants to Give Our Youth a God-Believing Education Free from Christian Subversion — 53

13. German Belief in God is Only a Religious Concern of Germanic Peoples — 55

FOREWORD

With youthful enthusiasm and conviction we announce the will to believe in God, and carry faith into the self and fight for it. We must always be clear to ourselves from where this faith flows and from what eternal reasons our inner life is fed.

This writing calls for a contemplative stop. It wants to consolidate and strengthen us in the German belief in God and grant us security in our faith, a foundation. But it should also be our armamentarium and weapon in our fight for our German faith and the future of our people.

The German faith still lives on in times of struggle and war. Adherents must be mindful of both at the same time: breaking into the enemy's front and solidifying and deepening the convictions one's inner self, that they may be untouched by any faith but one's own.

The statements outlined on the German belief in God are not a confession in any form. German belief in God is not limited to the letter, it lives from the eternal order of God as it is shown in nature and human life, in history and the fate of the Germanic peoples. The German belief in God does not live from the unique revelation of a God, which is supposedly attested in a "holy scripture", but from the constant testimonies of God about us, around us and in us.

1. The Main Focus of the German Belief in God, is God.

The German belief in God lives, stems from the eternal, stems from God.

Behind all reality stands the power of God.

German belief in God knows man has an entrance and exit, and does not hold the course of his life in his own hands, but that his coming and going is subject to the eternal laws of becoming. German belief in God does not presume to fully recognize the order in which all living things stand or to comprehend the laws according to which life comes into being and is perfected down to their ultimate basis, but it is an inner certainty - just a certainty of faith that the individual life is part of the eternal connection of all events. German faith gives man the certainty that he lives in an order that supports him just as securely as the shining star in the infinite distance and like the flower at his feet. And this order of God is sacred to him. We humans have to give our ideas and our inner experiences names if we want to communicate them to others, this is what the law of our spirit wants. We people of German belief in God give this ever-supporting ground in which we rest the name with which the religious person always designates that unrecognized supreme thing that fills him with reverence: the name of God.

For German belief, God encompasses the infinite fullness of all events, the whole order of the world. God is in the becoming and growing of the cell into leaf and blossom and fruit, God is in beauty as well as in joy, God speaks through eternity of our blood, God is in the awareness of our self in the depth of our soul.

God is the infinite whole in which we live. Every glimpse into nature, every quiet contemplation of the infinity of stars, the inquiring look into the secret universe of the cell, like the knowledge of the stream of heredity, flowing from eternity to eternity is an astonishment at the order, the expediency and necessity in existence. Every amazement in life is an experience of God.

If you look up and down at the heights and into the depths, at the praising stars in the sky, the surging sea and forest and field, there you see God everywhere. And the same God dwells and is enthroned in you also, for everything is God's and is of him. And if you don't meet him in all nature around you and in the depths of your heart, you will never experience him and know of him. And there is only one book in which you can read of him: "that is, the world around you and within you." (Jacob Böhme).

German belief in God does not speak of a God who was devised by people in a dispute over words, but of the living God who lives within our amazement, in our joy, in the beautiful and powerful in nature, who emerges from the order of the world as a whole, speaks to us, who reveals himself in the fate of the individual, as in the history of the volk, who is meaning and greatness in all that is spiritual, like the breadth and depth of our knowledge.

Experiencing God is always a process in our inner experience. And everyone has this experience in their own way. But since this experience of the divine belongs to the human psychic world as an awareness, it also depends on the psychic nature of the human being. And so German belief in God is the way we feel the Germanic-Nordic Soul attitude deals with the powers of life, and seeks God in the reality of life.

With the question of God, German belief in God wants to find a way to the ultimate reality, to ultimate originality, to a profound understanding of life and existence. This comprehension is not an understanding in the sense of thinking, but an inner being grasped by the certainty that all unrest flows from a calm, that what is striving for divergence wants to find its own center again, that what has been separated rushes towards unity and all tensions demand to be resolved in a balance, to hasten new tensions. For the deepest meaning of life for the Germanic-Nordic people is the struggle. As he asserts himself in battle and fate, in victory and defeat, he finds and lives his God. God is to him like an inner loyalty to life, even to its ambivalence. God is the affirmation of the last, even the most bitter, that comes our way. Anyone who has found this, yes, lives from the eternal, grounded. But this reason is not given to us in a word or in a scripture, but is a certainty gained through struggle and self-reflection. In this belief, the emotional-spiritual faculties inherent in our race and our blood rise to the guiding forces of inner life and physical action.

However, we must reject the opinion that God is nothing more to us than a simple word as a misrepresentation of our religious concern. Our sacraments lie in our deepest contemplation. Our belief in God is neither a mental nor an emotional gimmick. We are deadly serious about our faith.

Because man needs the certainty of standing in God's order in order to find a clear path through life, in order not to despair in pain, to show the right bravery in the code and courageously to take up the fight with all the powers of life. According to German belief, God is not a being frozen into a person. Perhaps it is in the raffish nature of some people that they need such a judging and punishing material being to lead their lives. The Germanic-Nordic man becomes in the man who wants to be led or must be led. In the brave person who trusts himself and lives in reality with open minds, clear eyes and inner sincerity.

In the Germanic-Indo-European life of faith, the divine was always what was becoming, what was actively working, the will to live, the power flowing through all living things. Life itself with its coming into being and passing away, the world of the soul with its joys and sorrows and the realm of the spirit with its powers of knowledge and moral freedom are the loud witnesses of the eternal power of God.

If German belief in God does not separate the reality of nature and divinity, it lives with this connection between the spiritual and the natural, entirely out of the Germanic attitude of soul. In the oldest Germanic literature, which gives us an insight into the Germanic-Indo-European interpretation of the world and thus also into the basic religious ideas of our forefathers— the divine order and the inner structure of the world as a whole are seen in the image of a tree that nourishes its roots from a well, that nobody knows. The great German men of spirit and faith each called God by very different names, because he never showed himself to them as one unchangeable person, but always only as the creative, ordering and goal-setting power in the multifaceted reality. They speak of God-nature, God-infinity, God-freedom, God-mind and God-conscience.

It does not therefore require supernatural and merciful powers of cognition and a special "glorious light" to feel the work of God. He shows himself all over the world, we only need to look in and around us. German belief in God does not fight the spirit in God that works its way into this life from an unworldly hereafter through the mediation of church and priest. German belief in God does not adhere to the doctrine of the unique revelation of God in his Son, carried by Christianity into the Germanic world, and to the definition of this doctrine in a so-called "holy" scripture.

According to German belief, God is not the Jewish idol Yahweh, who does his will only made known to those who submit unto him. We do not invoke this Hebrew name in our invocation, even removed by centuries of subversion, it represents a foreign entity, not God. According to German belief in God, God, who made our volk, is the ordering power in the world, the eternal ground from which everything that happens flows. God works in life, in becoming, in will, in deed.

With the awakening of national self-confidence, the man of a German belief in God is given the task of leading life according to the morality of his race by putting it into helping action and fighting. Ever since we became human, the spark of God has rested at the bottom of our souls. To kindle it and bring its light into life, this is our task of faith.

But we are convinced and see it from the history of faith of the German people that this little spark of God that is within us does not come to us from outside and is not a part of an extra-mundane spirit that leans towards us from the otherworld far away, but that it is a soul-spiritual power in us, bound to our kind and in its special form is only our own. This little spark of God can only find the form that becomes the essential basis of our religion in our Germanic souls.

We don't want to go out and proclaim the German faith to the whole world. We couldn't do that because of the inner bond of faith in our species. But the German faith calls out to people of Germanic blood: Recognize yourself! Recognize your kind and learn to understand the voice of your blood and do not turn away when your innermost being, which is nothing other than the healthy, raffish human being within you, wants to open up to you! From your self-knowledge, from your loyalty to your own intuition, to your nature and to the racial basic forces of your soul, you shall receive the great good of a German belief in God!

That is the basic character of the German faith, that in the über-attunement which stands with the Germanic-Nordic soul attitude. The Christian Spirit-God is not given to us in the blood and in the creative disposition, but reaches into our life as something alien to life, something beyond the world. We attempt to reconcile it with our national spirit but its source material remains alien. A nature-bound feeling for life, however, can only ever see body, soul, and spirit as a whole, which does not only come together in life, but which is there at the same time as life. The Christian Spirit-God is only added to the assets of the races and peoples, because he is not tied to blood and kind. But this Spirit-God enthroned somewhere, who does not belong to the reality of the world, but has a special kingdom outside it, from where he communicates himself to men through revelation in the word or through the mission of himself as Christ, destroys the image of a unified grown and self-ordered reality. The spirit-world duality of Christianity, from which then flows the doctrine of man distant from God and his necessary salvation through the mediator, is opposed to the racially determined blood-spirit unity doctrine, according to which our nature is decisive for our experience of God.

In the Christian sense, religion lives in the realm of a spirit that is incompatible with the realm of nature. According to this view, there is no racial conditionality of belief, but religion is an affair in itself, raised above all blood ties, as kindred and "brotherhood in Christ". But according to

German belief, race is not only a bodily formation, but also a soul-spiritual content, and that is why it also determines the nature of his God-experience.

Now it is said that the German belief in God destroys the spirit and with it all the high values of human culture when it places God in the reality of life. But where is God more spirit, where, in the sense of the Christian church, questions are asked like: Is God a body? Is there a composite of form and matter in God? Is God quite simple? Does God make sense of himself? Or there, where we worship him as an active force, where we face the divine event with reverence and leave nameless what speaks to us from the depths?

This Christian Spirit-God, who is detached from all reality of life, cannot put down fine roots in the soul of the German man. It is not without emotion to follow how the German way of life made an effort over the centuries to incorporate this foreign teaching into its essence. Just as German blood was passed on to German blood, the German belief in God also passed through the centuries, misjudged and persecuted, also forgotten by the Germans themselves, but at times proudly and bravely raising their heads, never completely disappeared or destroyed. Where people lived in a German way, there was always the German belief in God, and where the German need was greatest, there the German belief in God always grew strongest.

God is at the heart of all life that is filled with duty and responsibility. Can such a life filled with God, with its belief in the God-human connection, be accused of deifying man in himself? The German belief in God has nothing to do with such human arrogance, it lives from the seriousness of the final obligation that rings out of its conscience. And in conscience, God himself rises up in us. Ultimately, however, conscience is nothing other than the "innocence of our found blood". And in this sense, i.e. in the sense of the exaltation of the natural and species given to the direction of our lives, in the German faith, God speaks from our blood.

How different that God who is bloodless spirit and around whom the doctrine of the personal and triune God was formed. This conceptual idea of God has never become the species image of the Germanic people. It came to us from abroad, it is so much a work of man and has emerged so much from human disputes about concepts and words, about doctrines and beliefs, that it must contradict a conscious German to regard this body of teaching as the only revealed religion. God reveals himself to us everywhere and constantly.

God does not speak to us from a doctrinal structure, but we can experience him from the fullness of life. God is as big and wide and light as deep and rich our inner life is. The way to God does not lead through a doctrinal building, nor does a confession give the certainty of his nearness, but only a rich inner life. Therefore we must listen to what is within us and take care that it speaks to us only from our own being.

How should a German man violate his freedom of thought and strangle the urge of his knowledge if he were to believe in the birth of a human being without conception, in the equality with God of this born human being, in his bodily resurrection from the dead and in his bodily ascension to heaven! And to spend his life reconciling it with the reality of the growth of his people, who are somehow less than this man! And how should he be able to realize from this belief that he can only find peace in his heart by accepting such exaggerations as true!

The fact that this belief or non-belief pronounced the verdict on the salvation or damnation of our people for thousands of years has brought so much hardship and destruction to Germany and its brethren. We are not pious when we hold teachings and views to be true, which human error has deliberately or unintentionally worked out, but when we willingly conform to the order of life. Life with its regulations, such as family, people and homeland, is willed by God. Wanting to become one with the meaning of these ordinances, that is living piously in God.

Descend into the law of our inner being and get the instructions for the work of the day from what is truly our own, that means going the way of religion. But this heart must flow as a clear stream of blood, and a pure attitude of soul must shine out.

We don't want to ask so much who has the right image of God in his heart or in his knowledge, but we want to live as if we have received the highest power of God, the living God. Let this inner certainty of ours flow in word and deed.

2. The German Belief in God, Wants the Unity of Our People in a Faith True to the Race.

German belief in God knows that the question of God as a religious issue is common to all people. But he also knows that faith only gives full spiritual security, only then can the power of overcoming and devotion flow out and become inner certainty when it is free from all alien things and lives completely and works from the strength of blood and racial type.

A belief can only then have ultimate certainty and inner support, given to all walks of life when he has the deepest and purest expression is our kind.

It would contradict the spiritual unity of the individual as well as the unity of the people if we built our way of life on the one hand on the strengths of our kind, on race, blood and soil, on people and homeland, but on the other hand on the one that binds us most deeply in order, even the order of our faith, based on teachings and beliefs which are foreign and not of our racial nature.

Race is a source of mental and spiritual powers and character values. These blood values are our most sacred folk-good. In large areas of life we allow the importance of hereditary factors to apply in practice, but we still want to exclude one area, that of religion, from this consideration. Germans still shy away from examining the values and beliefs that have hitherto been in force to determine whether they are appropriate to their species and are content to keep them as accustomed traditions. However, the racial-psychic consideration is also to be applied to the question of the origin of our beliefs. Folk feeling and folk spirit, belief in guilt and the experience of God have grown out of the intrinsic value of the race, which we cannot give up and let drown in foreign culture if we don't want to lose ourselves as Germanic-German people. Otherwise we would get lost in the innermost areas of the soul and spirit, in the religious, we would become broken and without peace. All men among all peoples seek the way to eternity, but the images in which eternity is seen, what speaks in man as duty and conscience are as different from one another as the law of blood, under which peoples and guilds stand.

It must not be the case that the social, pedagogical, or economic stratum of our community allows itself to be guided by the recognition of racial claims, while another, such as the religious one, excludes the validity claim of the racial from their sphere. The soul-spiritual layers of our national body touch and influence each other far too much for this to separate one layer from the other without endangering the unity and the found growth of the whole.

We are therefore convinced and live with the inner certainty that we will find true pioneers for the spiritual unity of our people if we stand up for a faith that is true to the species.

Standing on the basis of the National Socialist worldview, will our racial destiny also become our religious destiny, to which we commit ourselves out of inner responsibility and out of reverence before the commission that speaks to us from the eternal foundation of our people, our kind, and our blood. The race not only separates peoples from humanity and presents them as national personalities, but it also appears as a requirement to the peoples to remain true to their way. And that voice from the blood comes to us like the highest commandment of duty, to follow it is the task of our German faith.

The home of German belief in God is German soil. Where German people feel German and live from the depth of their kind, there is the holy land of German faith. And this holy land can only be called Germany.

Every racially healthy people must also strive towards a high image of its kind in the religious sphere.

Faith is a person's deepest concern. The German man must look fearlessly into this inner being. He must recognize whether the ultimate impulses for his thoughts and actions flow from his own convictions, or whether he is only guided by habit. The German man must live from the great bravery that only ascribes a right to faith that has been won through inner struggle and is therefore essential and unshakable to him.

Faith is only a truth and certainty when it is entirely our own, not tied to word and teaching, but nothing other than the deepest awareness of an order that runs through us, of a law of life in which we ourselves stand.

Life challenges us all, we feel that with every breath we take, with every dawning day, with every job that obliges us because it is wanted by the whole. This demanding life may not be heard by all as an inner voice, German belief in God, however, this call of life will flare up pure and compelling voice of blood.

The blood is the symbol of the bondage of German belief in life, as it rises every day and every hour from the eternal depths of human and ethnic order. The German faith that is true to the species is not difficult to acquire through teaching, it does not come through external gestures and not through illumination from above, but is the simply and simply experienced fact that we have found a secure footing in our existence if we bravely, faithfully and truly follow the high images of the German kind.

And even if a person's faith is a matter of deepest concern, then the true-to-type German faith, because it rests on the commonality of a blood and spirit connection, becomes a common experience of all who feel they are of the same blood. Species-faithful faith is not a possession to take pride in, it is a force that urges us to use our gift for our people.

We can cling our hearts to this belief more and more ardently, because it does not lead us away from the reality of life and from the connection with our people, but opens up to us more and more deeply the fateful connections with this people. And these connections were not thought up by people and are not thrown over us like a compulsion, but are an order of existence that is established from eternal grounds and is therefore the language of God himself. When it has become an inner certainty that the people are God's ordering thoughts, then living in this certainty means living in the German faith in God.

We want to have an effect on the people so that they have the courage to face up to themselves and dare to listen to the voice that speaks to them from the depths of their kind. Then in the restored glory of the kingdom there will also be a people upright and unbroken in their faith. In this people, who have also found their home again in faith, the racial idea finds its ultimate fulfillment and the people its unity also in the depths of the soul.

3. German Belief in God Requires No Mediation.

Since German belief in God receives divine mandate from life itself, since the experience of God is directly given to it from looking at the ordered world, as a whole, and from looking into the divine depths of the soul, it needs no mediator between man and God. God is not an extra-worldly power, but belongs to this world and is its innermost pulse. There is only one world reality that includes God, man and nature. The whole of the world is worked through by God. All life and its blossoming continuance is posited, divine order. The whole world moves in such an all-encompassing, cosmic order. Whoever serves this order, serves God. If we devote ourselves to maintaining this order in an active life, our life becomes a form of worship and we then are secure in this existence that is meaningful. In the deepest moments of this experience, we are filled with the feeling of being pious and close to God.

Since, according to the German faith, God has not imprisoned himself in the concepts of ecclesiastical teaching, nor has he withdrawn into an extra-mundane world, he does not need the priest as the representative of God and explainer of this teaching, and does not need the gradation of the means of grace that the priest in the church claims to administer.

German faith especially abhors the institution of auricular confession because it is ignoble of a Germanic person. The German man appears before his God as a free man. The German belief in God ascribes to man the ability to elevate himself to the divine if he so resolves, and that his good ultimately stems from the strength of his innermost nature.

For German belief in God, the attitude towards the divine is a question of attitude and character. Anyone who knows how to stand rightly for himself, also honors himself. And honor stems from brave and proud people, full of inner strength and bright joy of heart. Wherever there is honor in faith, there the great strength grows in us to struggle for the highest and ultimate questions, be it in victory or in defeat. We don't ask for mercy, we want to fight for the fate of our lives ourselves as free people, even if we know that this struggle for life often ends incomprehensibly to our own understanding.

After all, it is part of the nature of a Germanic human being that he does not want life as a gift, but as the price he has won for a free man.

The mediator and redeemer faith of Christianity is alien to the Germanic path. It does not belong to the basic religious forces of the German soul. Out of the feeling of security in the world, we do not want to be redeemed from life, but rather to be led more and more to a right life, true to our way. This self-reflection in style and faith does not require a mediator sent by God, but only loyalty to our own self and looking up to the German faith personalities who are erected like memorials on the millennium-long path of German faith and intellectual history. Any sacrifice made toward our ability to lead a righteous life, only stems from our own tributes to God.

How can there be a mediator between us and our blood, between us and our kind, between us and the God-power at work around us and within us!

Only a religion that knows no god within the world and one only outside the world, and therefore no faith bound by blood, can see man's sanctification in his redemption from this world and send him a mediator for this task, which is contrary to his healthy nature. Also the Germanic-Nordic people know of a "salvation" which they trust like an inner law and which they listen to as if they were an inner guidance. In being led to faith, the German man knows that he is blessed with this "salvation" when duty and loyalty, honor and pride find the root forces of his physical activity.

The German-Nordic people want to stand for themselves, even if this high level of self-confidence leads them to hardship and deep loneliness. In his destiny he fights for his self-assertion, even among the masses in life foreign to him. For him, going down fighting does not mean succumbing to weakness, but nevertheless being an example of the victory of a high, if hidden, meaning of life. The German hero hunter is a single triumphal prisoner of this self-assertion and this loyalty to oneself in the hero's downfall. Whoever has lost this attitude, let him descend again to the primal mothers of the German soul type. All born-again Germans, will then joyfully shape a life of faith himself.

4. German Belief in God Sees the Way of the Unity of Our People in Completely Overcoming Christianity.

Christianity as a pure spiritual religion is incompatible with overly ethnic attitudes. It is from Christianity that the word *ethnisch* (ethnic) was first derived, from those of our people who rejected this doctrine.

This foreign religion rejects any attachment to nationalities, regards them as secondary salvation. It is not national, but, true to its mission to spread all over the world, to each who is not "saved"— it is international. Because Christianity does not profess race as a specific soul-spiritual being, it also rejects the belief in the religious-creative ability of the soul of a solitary people. The Christian God, alien to life and beyond all reality, speaks the same word to all peoples through the unique revelation of a scripture. He doesn't ask whether certain peoples, being different species, might not have the capacity to absorb these supranational revelations, he doesn't worry about whether peoples from their innermost essential differences have to turn against him. Thus, over the centuries, in addition to the Christian attitude imposed on them by force and habit, the German people have repeatedly sought to form their own life of faith out of the forces of their own kind, and are too believers in doing so. These are experiences that are available to us today as a rich treasure of original finds and testimonies of a German belief in God. A religion is only a salvation for a villager to the extent that it calls upon the people's hereditary powers, strengthens their sense of morality and thus increases their strength, in this life or thereafter.

German belief in God is not based on the revelation taught by a church of a Spirit-God who is alien to life, even hostile to life, who only promises happiness and fulfillment to people in a far-off earth and otherworldly hereafter and thus takes life's meaning and its sanctification, the commitment stripped of his greatness and dignity for the prosperity of the people when he speaks of "his" kingdom, which is not of this world. The man growing out of German nature listens to life itself, for out of blood and earth form his body, and also his spirit, and his faith.

As much as the German who believes in God respects every honest conviction and sees the national community as an inviolable national goal, his German faith is also a great obligation for him to stand up and fight in order to prepare a foundation in the German people for him and his progeny.

It is a matter of course for him that Christianity should be, must be, completely overcome. The shape of this fight can only be in the creative work of building up the species-appropriate piety, less an argument with words, than a redesigning out of reflection on one's own racial type of soul. However, German Faith resolutely rejects unclear attitudes, such as those represented in a "German Christianity".

On the Christian side, an attempt is being made today to establish an inner relationship between Christianity and the German people. After Christianity in the spiritually awakened German people was forced to conceal its Jewish roots and therefore suddenly declared, "The Christian faith is the insurmountable religious opposition to Judaism," it now seeks to tie a spiritual bond between itself and the awakened German. It seeks to trick the German soul into believing a break in the oral traditions of the Jewish books with the rabbis of today. Just as in a Jewish Christianity, the Jewish Messiah was the religious longing to point to Christ, so now in the intention of a German Christianity the idea of light of the Nordic-German faith is supposed to have been laid out from primeval times on the birth of Christ. Christianity begins along with paying attention to the religious tendencies of the German soul. They are of a high enough nature to provide favorable soil for the seed of Christianity. But this recognition does not go so far that in the eyes of this German Christianity, the German people's native faith, which draws its ultimate depth from the religious formative powers of the Nordic race, could lead to an independent and self-contained contemplation of God. In doing so, Christianity forgets that this acceptance of Christian teachings has always only taken place in the form of a confrontation between the German species and itself. The Christian age in Germany was a German-style life with drifty forms, of which the Gothic cathedrals testify just as much as the pictures of Christ and the Life of the Virgin by Dürer. So-called German Christianity today presents the written proclamation as the answer to the religious questions of the pre-Christian German faith. The German, however, does not seek this answer for a strange reason. His faith rises from the depths of his own soul, through which he feels connected to the faith of his forefathers.

It is not the turning to the birth of the god's son that leads to the original home of the German faith, but rather the turning to our grasp in the worldview and God-view as it was attested to us in the religions of the Germanic Indo-European peoples. Life in the great and wide order of God fills us with such deep peace and joy that is so open to the world that nothing urges us to be assured of our nearness to God only when we receive it through Christian revelation.

Just as the Christian mission once covered up the religious customs of our fathers in the Christian sense and thereby crept into the hearts of the Germans, so today the "German Christianity" tries to establish the "Christian light in the

Nordic-German country" by implying that the spark of the Aryan religions are mere forerunners to this belief in Christ. That the Jewish messiah prophecy was meant to align with the heroes of our people. We want to be vigilant against such attempts at a renewed uprooting of the German soul, which uses well-known means to convert and reinterpret beliefs that are true to the species, into Christian tenets.

Because it is simply no longer possible for a German today to find a Christianity with Jewish roots, and because the light of life of Christianity would go out in the German area, "German Christianity" makes the discovery that from now on instead of Judaism, folklore is to be made the basis of Christianity. "German Christianity" is thus trying to create a living connection between itself and the people's beliefs, so that Christianity no longer appears alien to Germans who think in a very fishy way, and according to their species, to live. Traditional faith becomes undeveloped Christianity, Christianity the fulfillment of the faith of the forefathers. After a "German Christianity", the volk-faith carried and nurtured Christianity as if it were in a mother's womb until it was able to appear as an independent religion. This is intended to prepare the ground for the formation of popular Christianity, inextricably linked with Germanness. The supranational status of Christianity appearing superficially abolished, anyone who should still get the idea of standing up for the development of a German, species-appropriate worldview and God-view would be declared an enemy of the people, because now proof of a lack of Germanness would be taken in not being a Christian!

The German belief in God, however, seeks God in the many forms of His revelations, but it does not seek Jesus Christ, or those foreign scriptures from which he was devised.

For the German belief in God it is therefore also completely immaterial whether Christ was an Aryan or a Jew, whether he is to be regarded as a historical figure or as a timeless mythical phenomenon. These controversies should not concern the believing Christians either, since Christ is the Son of God for them, and therefore as a divine being must stand above all humanity. The German faith certainly appreciates the appearance of this Jesus Christ within certain religions of broader humanity, but since this founder of the religion belongs to a foreign species, neither his word nor his personal appearance can become an obligatory model for our inner being. German belief in God seeks its role models and leaders from all areas of Germanic Indo-European religious and spiritual life. The Germanic does not fear that the possible similarity of the figures could confuse him; the deep power of faith inherent in the race speaks to him precisely from the richness of the leaders and heroes. Who a person takes as his or her belief and life model is his innermost concern, but if Aryan blood flows through these high and noble people and if they are living disciples of our spirit, then the multitude of these religious leaders will only deepen our experience of God and let us recognize more and more clearly the essence of Germanic God vision and morality.

We do not consider a renewed acquisition of Germanness to be beneficial, albeit de-Jewish Christianity, nor vice versa a further Germanization of Christianity, but we can only see the religious salvation of our people in a true-to-species belief.

Even a so-called "German Christianity", which wants to be freed from all ties to Rome and Jews, stands as a foreign body among Germans because of its historical origins and its intellectual content, which as a religious expression of a species image that is foreign to us will never find German roots. Soul, the German faith, as the inner certainty from the eternal foundation of blood and the way of life, is what is most peculiar and genuine of the people.

The roots of our faith lie in the depths of our own souls. Here is our inner home. If we feel secure in this ground, then we also look at the foreign and try to understand it. But German belief in God will never go the way which a "German Christianity" tries to grant to the German volk: to look for one's own being in the foreign.

The attempt to find a German-völkisch root for Christianity should be done away with once and for all. If it can no longer draw its strength from within itself, then it should not graft itself onto someone else's orchard to stimulate new blossoms. This procedure must be recognized as makeshift, disingenuous, one that will ultimately fail as time passes, and one which will gradually weaken those who attempt in err to sustain it.

The path to the great goal of seeing the German people united in faith cannot be achieved by half-measures and ambiguities. This includes a clear focus solely on our racially determined soul.

We Germans who believe in God want to go our way bravely and faithfully follow our path, and live our German belief in God with the personal courage to pray.

5. The German Belief in God Stands in Awe of Death.

The German belief in God does not try to hide the natural fact of death by meagerly suggesting eternal happiness in the afterlife, but recognizes dying as a given fact. A beauty of nature from which we cannot escape, not even by means of a Christian doctrine of immortality. But even with this natural attitude toward death, dying is not an easy thing, and dying is often harder than is commonly stated. We mustn't close our eyes to the fact that in most cases life is harsh, that very often it comes to an end without all our questions having been answered and that death stands in the middle of this tragedy of life. But only when we face life in this way does it make sense to speak of heroism and the courage to make sacrifices, of loyalty to life even in the harshest of fates, as values of the German way of life.

If man's self-assertion in heroism and loyalty is to become one of the highest values of German faith, then we must recognize life in its hardships and understand it as man's struggle with the powers of the earth. Only in death do we show ourselves in our full greatness - and yet helplessness in the void.

Even if we understand death as a natural occurrence and can talk about it in words, we still haven't gained anything for our inner attitude and way of life. Death must be received as a very large and voluntary acceptance in the source of faith from which we draw life, then inner peace and security will come over us from which we can find satisfactory answers to the last questions that mankind has always asked and will never stop asking. These questions which also arise in the soul of the German people: the questions of death and immortality.

Thoughts about death are a fundamental religious desire of mankind. In its position on this question, however, German God-belief does not want the answer to be simply given and forced in some finality, but rather to approach the solution from our point of view.

Death itself gives us no answer to our questions, the dead remain silent. But that's why we don't want to wrap bloodless fantasies around the event of death, which should obscure the fact of death for us, but we want to grasp death with a brave heart, like the Knight, [Death and the Devil] by Dürer, where it can be grasped by human means of knowledge and there linger in silence again. Its ultimate meaning is hidden from us, it still owes us the ultimate answer to our questions.

Death belongs to man's destiny, because man is nature, and nature reveals itself in life as in death. However, man is not just pure, unconscious nature, he is nature that has risen into conscious, spiritual life. The animal may die somewhere in the quiet, forgotten by its fellows, but in the case of humans, death will always be accompanied by the pain of some separation, some disturbed community. When death takes hold of a person, a being, a personality will always leave us, with its unspeakable invisible threads of love and loyalty, friendship and camaraderie– to parents and siblings, to family and children, to clan and tribe to which the whole community of the people was attached.

If we only look at the great universe and at the eternity of time, then the death of men is nothing other than the fall of the leaves on the earth in autumn. But if we consider that human beings live in communities that bind people together inwardly, then death does not occur in human life, only a natural way back into the womb of mother earth, but it is experienced as a violent detachment from a community of soul and spirit.

This pain, which flows from the feeling of being suddenly alone, is real and sacred to German belief. We do not want to exaggerate this pain, which is humanly justified and natural. It is a holy sacrifice, which we mean, brings death.

As sacred as this lamentation and the pain for the dead is to us, German belief in God does not want to consume itself in it, but rather find its way through the event of death to belief in life and to an inner grasping of the divine order, in which life and death are sides of one and of the same event. German belief in God does not, like Christianity, glorify death, for which a dying person became the highest symbol and the most worthy of worship. Christianity carries the image of death into the corner of every house, and where the living God speaks the eternal language of the mountains, there the Christian church places the sign of death by the way. Isn't that almost like playing with death, and degrading the life we've been given, not to darken it with the shadow of death!

In the Christian conception, death, the dissolution, at the end of our attitude, and life, which stands before us as a tangible task, are set aside as intrinsically untrue and worthless. In the Christian view, only death is powerful, life is powerless, and where it presses and storms in us, where it sets goals for us and demands high things from us, that is precisely where, according to the Christian conception, things become most questionable.

The religious must have the whole of life as its background. A religion that makes death its teacher and disciplinarian violates life, and another that does not want to see death in life would studiously become a religion which does not want to embrace those experiences that nature forces upon us. In both respects, the one-sidedness of the attitude would mean that man would lose essential guiding forces for his inner formation. He would stagger to and fro helplessly and as if frightened when the forces of life or death claimed him and he hadn't reckoned with them in his time. We just don't live life alone, just as we don't put our lives in fear under the "remembrance of death", but seek to stand securely in God's eternal order, which confronts us in the alternation of life and death.

Let's not get too loud in our lamentations about the dead, there can be so much selfishness and complacency in this lamentation, which, moreover, no longer benefits the dead. If we become quiet before death, then we serve life and God's order greater. Life and death are inextricably linked. In the eternal alternation of becoming and dying, we alone experience life. The side of life that shows itself to us as God will always remain the most enigmatic to us, as, for us all life is bound up with consciousness, and consciousness ceases in death. Thus death becomes an end for man, an extinction, an annihilation.

A religion like the Christian religion, is pure in spirit, so that people are completely torn from their connection with the forces of nature that work in them and help determine their nature. For this they will see in death something alien, unnatural and worthy of a curse in final judgment.

First of all, death is an end. Our senses, which cannot be deceived, show us the dissolution of a human phenomenon with the onset of death. German belief in God does not conjure up wishful thinking in order to tell people about this to deceive perceptible facts, it does not appeal to human weakness but to inner bravery, it calls for recognition and challenges the hardships of life.

Death is not the surprising intervention of an alien violence. It is not the work of a devil or any evil person. German belief in God does not relate death to a person's physical behavior. Death comes to us all, whether we walk under the sun as good or bad people. Death is therefore not "the wages of sin", nor a punishment for human imperfection. It is as much a natural occurrence as all dying and forgiveness of animals and plants.

We must first recapture this natural meaning of death in order to lose the fear of death that is abused again and again. Because the fear of death is artificially nurtured in order to hand people over again and again to the hands of the priest, who promises the frightened people who are no longer sure of themselves redemption from this fear of death through the means of grace of the church.

We want to pursue the high goal of dying in peace with death in a natural way that lets us be true to our Germanic Nordic way. It also seems to us that our way demands pride and bravery from people, that is, it raises and forces the inner strength. The German belief in God opposes any intention of first suspecting and frightening the attitude towards life in order to then save the human being through priestly intervention as if from above. The feeling of security in the world, which makes us feel secure and calm inside, will also take away our fear of death, which is increased to an unnatural state by the Christian conception of life as a place of sin, and the associated threat of punishment in the afterlife.

The questions of death and immortality will never stop preoccupying people, including people who believe in German God. How we come to terms with these questions will reveal the nature and strength of our faith. We want to live on this earth and serve our people in such a way that we can stand before our kindred in the hour of death and do not need to be comforted by a promise of perfection in the hereafter.

We don't want to strive for immortality, which runs counter to all natural experience and which wants us to lead a completely life-alien existence in the afterlife as bloodless angelic souls. We only know a life that is tied to physical being. A bodiless existence cannot be grasped with the means of our cognition. Should we allow ourselves to be distracted from the tasks that visible and tangible life demands of us every day by looking at such an imaginary nothingness? Death and the thought of immortality call to us: Remember that you shall live!

We strive for immortality, which we can already have in this temporal life and which stands before us as a task that we are constantly trying to solve. And this task means: perfection and ever more progressive and clearer clarification of what we should be. What tremendous work everyone has to do on themselves and their people if the talents and strengths of our species are to be brought to the highest level! Only when this moral task should have been exhausted would it be time to approach the concern for a future life

If the immortality of which Christian doctrine speaks really, and quite certainly, carries within itself the fullness of happiness, then the true Christian should strive only for this immortality. But even the Christian seems to regard this immortality only as the object of a doctrine that teaches him bound by faith, but does not determine his way of life. He also strives for earthly goods and does not give up his life voluntarily in order to enjoy the bliss of eternal life as early as possible. For him, too, the law of life is higher than belief in this immortality, which is why even the Christian person is forced by life to take the guiding forces for his thoughts and actions from this life itself and not to an unimaginable, contrary to nature sacrifice immortality.

How much nourishment does this belief in immortality, which promises happiness and peace, compensation and retribution in a world beyond, receive from the inadequacy of human institutions! So let's do our part to alleviate social needs, let's work for our people's winter relief organization, look after mothers and children, ensure that the children relax, build adequate and healthy homes and give every working German enough leisure time to relax and celebrate: and we build on the prerequisites for a found and happy view of life and meet that worldview born of worry and need, which, from its earthly loneliness, is dependent on the comforts of an otherworldly immortality in heavenly happiness.

We hear it said that we set life too high and thereby rob man of the capacity for sacrifice. It is true that all life becomes futile and loses its great momentum if it were to lose the spirit of sacrifice, if life became so dear to us that we could no longer voluntarily give it up for a greater and higher cause. But German belief in God knows nothing of such idolatry of life. He only sees a hostile turn against life in the Christian glorification of death, and life is simply the arena on which we have to prove ourselves.

In the German belief in God, life and death enter into a reconciliation, for both phenomena of existence rise out of an eternal source. Man stands between the powers of life and death. He is formed by them. How he is affected by both determines the depth of his life.

The heroes of German legend and history, of which the dead of the World War and the dead of the movement are living witnesses, who did not dare the last thing out of monastic sentiment, but out of the bravery of their hearts and out of faith in life. They gave their lives so that the people could forever live.

Can the human personality be saved only by believing in an afterlife, as the Christian attitude claims? Must we sink down to the instincts of the beast if the earth gives us our task and not the sky? Only from the wholeness of his being, from his bodily and mental faculties, both of which go back to blood and race as their common ground of life, does man grow up to the high image of a personality.

Death does not destroy this image of a high humanity. The German personalities, as the clearly formed figures of men and women of our people, rise up from the earliest times of our history and are present to us. They live in their immortality.

It is completely unimaginable how in an eternal hereafter, which is only inhabited by pure angelic souls and therefore no longer knows any bodily forms, the human personality should continue to live and even rise to its perfection there! The whole body and soul of the human being is in this torn apart from the heavenly afterlife. How could there be a personal survival in him! Man cannot experience personality in any other way than that it is not bound to a human form, even the highest spiritual personality is at the same time flesh and blood.

But the immortality of the afterlife knows no survival in human forms. There will be no eating and drinking, no loving and free, just a union of disembodied souls finding bliss in beholding God.

To the extent that the Germanic-Nordic belief in immortality has come down to us, it shows itself to be full of blood, fighting for life and without any weariness with life. The dead sit together in the mound of death and, as ancestors, protect the living of their clan. In the Edda, the fallen man continues to fight as a follower of the dead god until one day he sets out with him for the last decisive battle against the powers of darkness. The death of the Jomsvikings will still be a deeply moving example for us to die bravely out of Germanic experience.

In the position towards death we must come to very clear decisions. When man comes into being, he rises up out of the bloodstream of his people. As a unity of body, soul and spirit he emerges from the darkness of eternity, and when his time has come this eternity takes him back again.

What entered visible life as an undivided whole is now to separate in death into the body, which disintegrates, and into the soul, which gathers with other souls in a beyond that is alien to reality. Such an idea is not taken from natural experience. It stems from a belief that was hostile to this life, that saw no more tasks on this earth and therefore had to console ourselves with the promise of an immortal life in the bliss of a heavenly bliss.

According to this belief, the body is only a temporary covering for the spirit, which in death frees itself from this bondage in order to be absorbed again in God.

The German belief in God finds God in the world and in the host of life. It is about struggling for immortality on earth. It is important to arrange our life in such a way that we do not need to be ashamed of it, that it would be valuable enough to enter immortality. With this belief in immortality, which places the highest demands on human self-improvement, we are again in a living relationship with the belief of our fathers, which says in the Edda:

> "Property dies, clans die, you
> yourself die like them.
> One thing I know lives forever: the
> glory of the dead man's deeds."

And yet another immortality stands high and sacred before a professor of German belief in God: His eternal survival in his children, in the bloodstream of his people.

In this way, the thought of death and immortality will not burden our minds, but inspire us to achieve the highest level of our destiny and to do our utmost for our people.

6. German Belief in God Opposes the Doctrine of Original Sin.

German belief in God opposes the doctrine that everything natural is good and bad. Every healthy and natural person feels a pang of uneasiness at the thought that the most tender human relationship, that of mother and child, could be tainted and disfigured by sin. What serves life, what belongs to its order and preservation, is neither good nor bad nor fruitful, this is necessary and natural and therefore sacred to natural feeling. We do not join in with the priestly religion's cry that the world is in trouble. This complaint is as old as the priests themselves. We want to use our talents, develop them and use them to the fullest. In this way we believe that we are serving the idea of the victory of good in the world most faithfully. And we don't see this highest good in some thought-up doctrine, but in the very close task of staying true to oneself and doing all we can for the honor and freedom and prosperity of the people.

We want to face our fellow countryman as our neighbor giving and fulfilling the tasks that the day sets for us; we believe that this is the best way to serve the Eternal.

We do not ask where our moral disposition for good comes from, we simply feel it as the voice of our blood and as the will of our kind we know only that we have to promote it through commitment and sacrifice.

Out of inner freedom man builds his character and shapes his destiny. He is not burdened by an original sin, but within the limits of his talents and strength he rises to a free, moral personality.

German belief in God does not see the suitable basis for a life of self-responsibility and creative joy in the doctrine of original sin. On the other hand, it gives the German people joy and strength to live their life out of the certainty of their hereditary nature. Belief in this inner nobility of the German kind does not make life easier or lessen responsibility; rather, it sharpens one's conscience and calls for deeper commitment. The doctrine of original sin is associated only with ideas of punishment, depravity and evil, the thought of hereditary nobles, on the other hand, gives the soul hope, impetus, strength and releases all the powers of self-responsibility and self-education. Where the German man becomes entangled in guilt, there he will acknowledge it and accept its consequences. This is the Germanic attitude. Here, too, German belief in God wants to call for self-reflection and self-liberation, in order to break the power of the priests over the German conscience.

7. According to the German Belief in God, the National Community is the Highest and Only Community—Rejecting any Clergy or Priesthood.

In German belief in God, the experience of God is determined by the racial type. It is a basic Germanic religious attitude not to grasp God as a concept of thinking and then to include him in a theological science, but to experience him everywhere in the world in his work and form. Man is not alien and lost in the face of this divine ground, but feels filled with this power that works in him, molds, and shapes him. The Germanic human being has always come to the experience and certainty of a force that carries all life and existence eternally on these two paths: the wide, anticipatory view of the world as a whole and the reflection on his inner soul, which he sees as the last order of all existence recognized and assigned the name that seemed to him to be the most exalted for this deepest concern of mankind: God.

According to German belief, God is the ultimate experience and the innermost experience. A personal, otherworldly god that cannot be experienced in the human soul is the idea of a foreign race. In order to expand such a view of God into a doctrine of God, to proclaim it and to make it understandable to people despite their alienation from life, the church needs a priesthood. But German belief in God does not need a priesthood, which acts as God's ambassador or proxy on earth, and does not need any ecclesiastical means of grace in order to climb a proverbial ladder to God with the hand of the Church. The German man rejects a priesthood that wants to bind the conscience and gain power over his convictions and inner being.

8. The German Belief in God Professes the Morality of Duty and Proves Itself In Service to Our People.

Every belief must carry within itself the power to create and lead a life. German belief in God also proves itself in German morality. Their deepest idea is the belief in the ability to take responsibility for oneself and to be free to make one's own decisions. In free choice, the true-to-species human fights for the values of his life, for home and fatherland, for loyalty and honor, for justice and high truth, in which divine demands are opposed to him become present. He follows the voice of his conscience, from which the consciousness of the species speaks to him as it fittingly should. The German man would rather give his life than do even the slightest thing against his conscience, or allow those corrupted and fallen from God's grace to taint it.

German belief in God does not need the fear of a punishing God to encourage moral action. He does not show willingness to help out of command to avoid hellfire or the hope of some eternal paradise, but rather this is a moral imperative for him. Life in struggle and commitment for the good and light, for homeland and nationality, for the service of the whole, forms the people of German faith to an internalized responsibility.

German belief in God does not look for humanity to prove itself, but the volk. From the depths of the Eternal the volk rise again and again as an entity formed by racial forces of soul and spirit within the order of nature. In this way the nation becomes a community of the same inner nature. The bondage appears most visibly in the nation and family. These forms of community speak clearly and obligingly of the divine order that prevails in these bonds of blood.

Seeing and understanding our way of life and forming the inner conscience out of our feeling for the way of life and tackling the tasks of life, that is German belief in God from our blood. From German belief in God we want to awaken to the response to our racial species image.

In this way, the German belief in God helps people from the moral and religious point of view.

9. German Belief in God Includes a Belief in Fact That Finds Visible Expression in the Way of Life.

Even if the German belief in God has to be conveyed through the word, since it wants to communicate itself to people, it is already pushing out of its roots, which are called life and blood and race, towards living representation in values of character and in enthusiastic, creative action. We want to stand firm and secure on this earth and look around for the tasks that will help us grow and mature. Innate in our people, we hear the call of that volk intrudes upon our conscience. No hope of the hereafter should divert us from our service to the people or even share our strength. Our German belief in God should not express its existence in prayers and should not be exhausted in teachings and formulas, but should prove its inner strength in the practical way of life, in the work of the day, in loyalty to the work and in committed camaraderie. German belief in God finally wants to drive out of the German people the dual nature that is committed half to the church and the other half to the people; it wants to give the German people a clear inward orientation and convince them that faith and people come from a single origin. Reasons grow, and this reason is the soul = spirit form of our racial kind. Worldview and faith are formed from this volkisch reason for life. From the knowledge of the indestructibility of these forces of blood, soul, and spirit, we step into life to deed and work and elevate this knowledge and this life into the inner experience of our German belief in God.

10. German Belief in God Recognizes Divine Work in the History of Our People and Builds on the High Images of the Germanic Race.

According to German belief in God, the volk are not an accidental historical phenomenon that entered historical time without meaning and without a mandate and could therefore also disappear from it again without becoming guilty. The volk is not an accident, it is the given of the divine will to live a racial destiny in this way and no other way. The people have a mission to fulfill that comes from the nature of their species given and that in the stream of fine blood from mythical times, emptiness circling in him. German belief in God does not live the history of its people as an event that is triggered and shaped by external political ties and impulses, but history is for him the formation and transformation of the German soul.

He can therefore only take his models for German humanity and German morality from German and related history.

Native German piety is not determined by the life and words of a donor. True-to-life German belief in God stands in living relation to the overall history of the German people. Where German manner and character speak to us from the past and present, there flow sources of German belief in God. In myth and fairy tale, in legend and history, in the realm of thought and research, of knowledge or of artistic design, the men of combative commitment inspire us or the figures of the quiet, contemplative introspection lead us to the depths. German belief in God builds on the confessions of German leaders and masters and finds inner strength. We are so rich in leaders and heroes, in fighters and brave sufferers that we do not need to have so-called role models imposed on us from abroad.

There have been German confessors at all times in German history, even in the centuries when powers alien to the faith sought to fundamentally transform the German soul. These men and women, in whom their German, ancestral nature always broke through, — often only after severe inner struggles, become high images for us to align ourselves with. We try to understand them when they reawaken the folkish way buried under foreign influences, we go with them in the fight for freedom of conscience and belief.

They become our masters in spiritual discipline and guides to the souls' unity.

Partly there are figures like Arminius, Widukind, Bach, Beethoven, Nietzsche and others, who through their inner inflexibility, despite the hardship of their lives, become models of German greatness, partly there are poets and god-founders, artists and seers, who represent German god-manhood and express Nordic lifestyle in their works. They all stood as creative people in German history and eat away at the bloodstream of the German people. In the form of legend and history, they took part in the German tragedy and became admonishers and shapers of German belief in God.

In the centuries when the Christian world of ideas ruled over the Germanic peoples, the Teutonic German way always resisted the foreign. The call for faith true to the species has risen from the German soul ever since it was forbidden to live from its own life. Standing up for the German faith in God is therefore not an ahistorical reverie and not an arrogant delusion.

The German belief in God is rooted deeper and longer in the German whole than the drifting foreign belief. The German belief in God, however, is part of the Germanic-German spirit and history of faith, which leads up from prehistoric times for the reasons of Germanic belief and extends through the Reformation and the Enlightenment and through the forms of German idealism to the belief of our age. German belief in God is part of the overall history of the German people; it finds a Germanic way of contrasting with the Christian foreign doctrine, which the German way first had to put on like a cloak if it wanted to gain acceptance among Germans.

What once counted as belief, as thinking and as a moral way of life among the Germans was fought by Christianity, which therefore did not tie in with the constructive forces of the German soul. German belief in God, however, wants to pull out of obscurity the buried and dishonored heritage of faith of the fathers and bring to light again the living threads between then and now that were never severed. Thus German belief in God reaches for living together, between the life of the faith of our fathers and searching for the answers of our time. It forms and sharpens the German conscience by uncovering the destructive effect of foreign mental influence on the history and fate of the German people.

Thus, in the German belief in God, past and present resonate together in the defense against spiritual infiltration by foreigners and are found in the prospect of the high images of the German kind.

A basic attitude towards life and a soul connects past and present, true to the species law of the indestructibility of racial values.

11. German Belief in God Strives for the Celebration of Faith in Naming Ceremonies, Marriages, and Honoring the Dead.

In the organization of celebrations, the German belief in God wants to unfold its inner strength. The German belief in God wants to manifest in the life of the people, as well as in that of the family life. The strong desire of all the people who have left the church for a deepening of their everyday life and for a festive and solemn highlighting of the stages of life requires the organization of celebrations and ceremonies. If this feeling for the solemn emphasis of the heyday of life were not followed, these folk comrades would succumb to a feeling of spiritual emptiness and desolation. Even the Christian faith recognized the eternal timelessness of pagan traditions and sought to claim them. Our people now seek to be bound to the religious values of our Germanic roots. In this way, the organization of festivals and celebrations becomes the deepest obligation to the individual comrade as well as to the entire volk.

No God-believing child should be born that is not deliberately placed in the circle of his clan and in the community of his people; no God-believing marriage should be contracted unless a husband and wife are just as solemn as they are in the bondage ring and friends take the vow of loyalty, to want to be new territory in the great kingdom of the people and to help build the eternity of the people through the holy will for the future in their children. And when we hand over a deceased person to the consuming flame or lower him into the bosom of the earth, then this last service takes place in a celebratory and dignified form, reverent to God's dominion over death.

12. German Belief in God Wants to Give German Youth a God-Believing Education in the German School Free from Christian Subversion.

German belief in God comes forth in life from the innermost depths of the German soul. It is therefore not easy to transfer, it is not something that can be converted to turnkey curriculum, but must grow from within every Germanic person and child. This innermost growth, conforming to the convictions of our species must be protected from external influences.

Since the German belief in God professes the racial laws of life, there can only be an education for it that is based entirely on racially intrinsic values. This education can only be provided by the German school without any Christian influence. It allows children to grow in their own strengths, which are inherent in their own way. Only this natural growth guarantees the unbroken, upright man, who is free and secure in his feeling for his species, who grows from his volk into his volk. On the way to such a growth that comes entirely from the basic forces of the German soul, the German youth will develop organically and unaffected and will finally be able to remain true to our people's internalized religious path.

Our schools must not hand over the young people to life, feeling impoverished and motivated by fear of reprisal, but must lead them to their people. It will stimulate the German child in depth and give him an attitude based on the powers of reflection, racial heritage, and folklore. And so, born of German blood and spirit, the young man will go about his work in service of his family and people.

The German belief in God does not see the teacher as a priest who educates German children on dogma, but as a gardener, a steward, an observer who explores growing life and knows how to promote it.

The Christian idea of education believes it is fulfilling a divine mandate when it tears apart peoples and invokes suspicion of their creative powers if they do not serve the priesthood's interests, when it trains the child into a type of human being that transcends the nation, when, to put it briefly, it educates them for the church and not primarily for the people and community. Education based on the German belief in God is based on the conviction that a people can only survive through the conscious promotion of their highest racial values and that this becoming a nation is a challenge formed from the eternal basic forces of our species.

13. The German Belief in God is Only a Religious Concern of the Germanic Peoples. It Respects Every Religious Conviction that Honors this Respect.

The German belief in God is concerned with only the ultimate experience and the security of the Germanic peoples within the broader order of the world as a whole. It calls upon the German people to recognize the deep forces of their souls, in order to come to the Germanic contemplation of God. If German belief in God also turns against other beliefs, then it has no intention of disrespecting people of other beliefs and thus endangering our national community, unless such beliefs intrinsically do such. Through such comparisons a God-Believer only wants to open one's eyes to the otherness and foreignness of faiths amongst our people. In this way, German belief in God, experienced in its depth, has an inwardly rousing effect and awakens in our people the reflection on their own soul-spiritual inheritance.

The German belief in God wants to rouse the lukewarm and strengthen the weak so that the folkish renewal and the National Socialist worldview find their ultimate depth and source of strength in a belief appropriate to their race.

Respect for every honest and strong conviction, even if it is not based on the German belief in God, is connected with this position on becoming a nation, also from the religious point of view. This respect for foreign beliefs is part of the essence of German belief in God, though it must remain on guard that they do not seek to turn our people against themselves. In the way we are a people, foreign faiths seek to turn us against each other. What a Goth once said to a Roman bishop: "Don't blaspheme the faith that you don't share, we don't blaspheme what you believe either!" This is also the guideline for German belief in God when dealing with people who think differently. German belief in God wants to primarily serve the national community, but that does not mean that the opposing views remain hidden, and that the German belief in God does not have to stand up and fight for what was recognized as true.

German belief in God wants to lead German people to the point where they recognize and feel their innermost core and elevate them to the certainty of a final and eternal experience that gives them strength in life and in death and for every good and noble deed in the service of God, as if from a foundation of God, people, and community.

A NOTE FROM THE EDITOR

The preceding pages were originally the second book in a series known as "The God Believing German", and were published by the National Ring of German God-believers (*Reichsring der Gottglaubigen Deutschen*).

These writings were a response to Kirchenkampf, as the clergy came at odds with the government and supporters of National Socialist Germany. Nevertheless atheism was regarded as synonymous with hubris and degeneracy, or the factions of the Communists to the East. Although only a small fraction of Germans identified as *gottgläubig* in a census of the time, the messages of these groups was broadcast by the RRG, state radio.

The notion that this religion of the Second World War was a new creation, created solely for political purposes, is only not entirely true. Today we know from scholarly research that pre-Christian European and Vedic scripture did refer to a God above the pantheons many refer to in mythology, a sky-father of many names, most prominently known as Dyeus Pater.

Other Historical Works on the Positive German God-Belief
Available wherever books are sold—

Bartsch, Heinz (1939; 2022).
The Positive German God-Belief.
ISBN 978-1-7370610-5-2.

Schulz, Karl (1939; 2023).
Content and Essence of German God-Belief.
ISBN 978-1-7370610-6-9.

www.ingramcontent.com/pod-product-compliance
Lightning Source LLC
Chambersburg PA
CBHW020133130526
44590CB00040B/605